Pam Scheunemann

Published by SandCastle™, an imprint of ABDO Publishing Company, 4940 Viking Drive, Edina, Minnesota 55435.

Printed in the United States.

Cover and interior photo credits: Corel, Corbis Images, Digital Stock, John Foxx Images, Photodisc

Library of Congress Cataloging-in-Publication Data

Scheunemann, Pam, 1955-
    Ch / Pam Scheunemann.
      p. cm. -- (Blends)
    Includes index.
    ISBN 1-57765-409-9
    1. Readers (Primary) [1. English language--Phonetics.] I. Title. II. Blends (Series)

PE1119 .S435 2000
428.1--dc21

00-033204

The SandCastle concept, content, and reading method have been reviewed and approved by a national advisory board including literacy specialists, librarians, elementary school teachers, early childhood education professionals, and parents.

Let Us Know

After reading the book, SandCastle would like you to tell us your stories about reading. What is your favorite page? Was there something hard that you needed help with? Share the ups and downs of learning to read. We want to hear from you! To get posted on the Abdo Publishing Company Web site, send us email at:

sandcastle@abdopub.com

About SandCastle™

Nonfiction books for the beginning reader

- Basic concepts of phonics are incorporated with integrated language methods of reading instruction. Most words are short, and phrases, letter sounds, and word sounds are repeated.

- Readability is determined by the number of words in each sentence, the number of characters in each word, and word lists based on curriculum frameworks.

- Full-color photography reinforces word meanings and concepts.

- "Words I Can Read" list at the end of each book teaches basic elements of grammar, helps the reader recognize the words in the text, and builds vocabulary.

- Reading levels are indicated by the number of flags on the castle.

Look for more SandCastle books
in these three reading levels:

Level 1
(one flag)

Level 2
(two flags)

Level 3
(three flags)

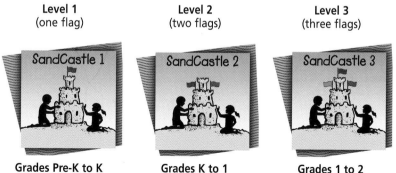

Grades Pre-K to K
5 or fewer words per page

Grades K to 1
5 to 10 words per page

Grades 1 to 2
10 to 15 words per page

Chad likes to have
some fun each day.

Chana and Chas like
to play checkers with
Uncle Chet.

ch

Chandler likes to play
fire chief very much.

Charlie and Rachel
like to watch the same
show.

11

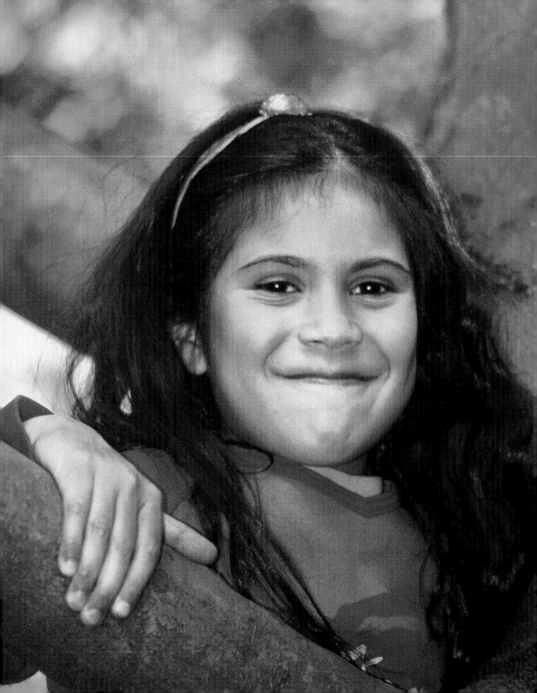

ch

Chelsa reaches the first branch.

She likes to climb trees.

ch

Chelsea and her chum chuckle at the beach.

Cherry sits in a big
chair on the porch.

17

Chip searches the
patch to choose the
best pumpkin.

Chyna eats lunch in
the kitchen.

What is for lunch?

(sandwich)

21

Words I Can Read

Nouns

A noun is a person, place, or thing

beach (BEECH) p. 15
branch (BRANCH) p. 13
chair (CHAIR) p. 17
chief (CHEEF) p. 9
chum (CHUHM) p. 15
day (DAY) p. 5
fun (FUHN) p. 5
kitchen (KICH-uhn) p. 21

lunch (LUHNCH) p. 21
patch (PACH) p. 19
porch (PORCH) p. 17
pumpkin (PUHMP-kin)
  p. 19
sandwich (SAND-wich)
  p. 21
show (SHOH) p. 11

Plural Nouns

**A plural noun is more than one
person, place, or thing**

checkers (CHEK-urz) p. 7   trees (TREEZ) p. 13

Proper Nouns

**A proper noun is the name
of a person, place, or thing**

Chad (CHAD) p. 5
Chana (CHAN-uh) p. 7

Chandler
  (CHAND-luhr) p. 9

Verbs

A verb is an action or being word

Adjectives

An adjective describes something

23

Match these ch Words
to the Pictures

cherry

watch

chipmunk

cheese

24